VEGAN

CW00450177

PREP FOR

BEGINNERS

The Starter Kit for Vegetarian Keto Life,

Weight Loss Solution with Cookbook and

Recipes.

Veganism with Ketogenic Diet Approach

and Plant Based Diet with Whole Food.

Table of Contents

© Copyright 2019 by Master Kitchen America - All rights reserved.

The following Book is reproduced below with the goal of providing information that is as accurate and reliable as possible. Regardless, purchasing this Book can be seen as consent to the fact that both the publisher and the author of this book are in no way experts on the topics discussed within and that any recommendations or suggestions that are made herein are for entertainment purposes only. Professionals should be consulted as needed prior to undertaking any of the action endorsed herein.

This declaration is deemed fair and valid by both the American Bar Association and the Committee of Publishers Association and is legally binding throughout the United States.

Furthermore, the transmission, duplication, or reproduction of any of the following work including specific information will be considered an illegal act irrespective of if it is done electronically or in print. This extends to creating a secondary or tertiary copy of the work or a recorded copy and is only allowed with the express written consent from the Publisher. All additional right reserved.

The information in the following pages is broadly considered a truthful and accurate account of facts and as such, any inattention, use, or misuse of the information in question by the reader will render any resulting actions solely under their purview. There are no scenarios in which the publisher or the original author of this work can be in any fashion deemed liable for any hardship or damages that may befall them after undertaking information described herein.

Additionally, the information in the following pages is intended only for informational purposes and should thus be thought of as universal. As befitting its nature, it is presented without assurance regarding its prolonged validity or interim quality. Trademarks that are mentioned are done without written consent and can in no way be considered an endorsement from the trademark holder.

Introduction

Congratulations on buying *Vegan Meal Prep* and thank you for doing so.

The following chapters will discuss not only the benefits of veganism but also how you can do it in a way that is good for your body and that will fit into your lifestyle without worry.

Veganism can be a big step for your diet and can be a daunting one. My goal in this book is to make it as easy as possible, with easy to follow recipes and constant reminders that you're really not missing out on all that much, especially when you consider just how amazing you will feel.

I've been doing veganism for a few years now, and I can barely remember what my life was like before it. I feel amazing, and my body is thanking me every single day. Your body will thank you, too.

This book is more than just slapping a bunch of vegan recipes together and calling ourselves a guide. This is a true guide to meal prepping and how it can help you stick to your journey into veganism and feeling good about yourself. Meal prepping is a powerful tool in any diet, and I think that anyone who wants to eat healthy while at the same time living in this crazy world of ours needs to learn how to do it.

There are plenty of books on this subject on the market. Thanks again for choosing this one! Every effort was made to ensure it is full of as much useful information as possible, please enjoy!

Chapter One: Going Vegan

Once you have decided to go vegan, it can be a little daunting. Also, a lot of people who decide to go vegan don't actually seem to know what this actually means.

A vegan diet means that you're involved with no animal products including meat, like beef, chicken, and fish, and dairies such as milk, butter, and cream. You're also not allowed eggs, which for many people is a breakfast staple. It can be very restrictive, and thanks to this, many people choose to opt out rather than cut out their favorites.

But the vegan diet can be incredibly rewarding when you do it right and you commit to it. Not only that, but even when all you want is a double cheeseburger with bacon, the recipes in here are all for you to meal prep, which will help you resist these cravings when they come.

But before we get into that, let's chat about all the benefits of the vegan diet, and more importantly, if it's right for you. First, let's start off with all the reasons why you might want to go vegan including health benefits, environmental benefits, and more.

It lowers your risk for type 2 diabetes and heart disease. These are two conditions that are very preventable, yet people keep getting them. On veganism, you're able to reverse a lot of the damage caused by foods with unhealthy high fat and carb content, lowering and even eliminating your risk for these diseases entirely. It also helps reverse conditions such as strokes, cardiovascular disease, high cholesterol, high blood pressure, and cancer.

You lose weight. The first time I ever met a vegan who had started recently (in his thirties); I asked him how it was going. He said he had lost 30 pounds in less than 5 months, all from making the switch. This is because the vegan diet is really focused on fresh, healthy foods with tons of nutrients. It's easy to overeat on animal products, and a lot more difficult to do that on the vegan diet.

You're showing compassion to the planet and other living creatures. This may be a factor for you, or it may not be. Veganism helps the planet in several different ways. For starters, it reduces your carbon footprint and your impact on climate change. It's been said that up to 51% of manmade pollution comes from the meat and dairy industry (this depends on the source). It takes an insane amount of fossil fuels and land to just house cattle. This will not only affect us in the future but dramatically impact wildlife. Not only that, but the animals are impacted as well. Corporations have done a great job in showing happy animals living on farms, but the reality is

pretty bad, with both the dairy industry and the

meat industry being equally to blame.

You really don't need animal products.

Despite what the industries would love to tell you, eating as much dairy and meat products as you do is actually...not...needed. You just need to look at our teeth to realize that our teeth are not actually made for eating meats, and if you can name another animal that consumes dairy after childhood naturally, I'll be very surprised. You really don't need it, and you can get all your nutrition from other sources. You just need to know how to do it right, and thankfully, this is what this book is for. Let's get started.

Going Vegan: Who Should and Shouldn't

When people go on the vegan diet, they automatically assume that it will immediately make them healthier and that they won't have to worry about keeping track of how much they're eating. This isn't true. The vegan diet only works if you're making sure that you're getting all of the nutrients you need, and this means that you have to do some careful planning. If you're someone who doesn't plan on filling your diet with a variety of healthy foods, meaning you're getting a variety of nutrients, the vegan diet is not for you.

Some people go on the vegan diet for all the benefits listed above, and they don't get anywhere. Why? Because they fill their plate with things like fresh fries and Oreos and pop tarts, all of which are vegan, and don't actually make the time to make sure they're getting a lot of healthy nutrients on top of this. Treating yourself in moderation is fine, but letting yourself run wild and just telling yourself "OK, no cheese, hamburgers, or fried chicken" isn't good enough. So, you really need to do it right.

Of course, we do have to acknowledge the fact that there are some potential risks that come with veganism, particularly in your nutrient levels. There are some nutrients that we can get from animal products, and you may find yourself needing to take natural supplements to help keep these levels up until you've found a balance that works. It can take time to adjust to a vegan diet, so keep these nutrients in mind:

Iron: Iron deficiency can be a problem for vegans as they're removing what is considered the highest source of iron, meat products, from their diet. Iron is also more easily absorbed into your body when you eat meat, as opposed to veggies. Basically, iron is lower in plant foods, and it doesn't absorb very well. So, be sure to seek out foods that are high in iron, and there's no shame in taking supplements.

Bone2: This is a tricky one, as this nutrient is only naturally found in animal-sourced products such as meat, fish, dairy, and eggs. Of course, these foods are off limits to vegans, but skimping out on your Bone2 can cause fatigue, appetite loss, and could even lead to severe neurological issues. But, bright side: a lot of products such as plant-based milks and soy products like tofu have a bone2, and supplements can be found quite easily at any drug store.

Calcium and Vitamin D: these two nutrients are often side-by-side in foods, and they're a two packaged deal. They both help with bone health and work together to keep them in good shape. If you skimp on one, the other will be affected. You must seek out foods and supplements with both of these things in them.

Omega-3 Fatty Acids: you need this nutrient for brain health, heart health, and even eye health. It also helps with inflammation, and unfortunately, the best sources are fish and eggs. Thankfully, this can also be found in many nuts and seeds, especially chia seeds, which you'll see a lot of in this book. Again, supplements are also an option.

It's important, at least for the first few months, to track and make sure that you're getting all the nutrients you need, and you're balancing out your meals. Be sure to always check labels and track your nutrients. Look up how much you need in a day and keep it varied. By keeping your diet full of variety every day, you're ensuring you're getting a variety of nutrients. And don't forget, there is really no shame in taking some natural supplements to help you along the way.

Speaking of nutrition loss, now we're going to talk about some mistakes you can avoid when going vegan.

Mistakes to Avoid

Everyone makes mistakes, but the key here is to list some that many people who are just starting out in veganism. If you can avoid these, you'll find that your life will be so much easier and the transition will go (a lot more) smoothly.

Not eating a variety. We already talked about this above, but I want to brush on it a little more, really emphasizing that this is important. When you're starting out, it's really easy to get stuck on what's easy or foods that you already know you like. You need a variety of nutrients, and you won't get this just from eating pasta with pasta sauce every night. It's easy, but you're not getting everything you need. That's why we're meal prepping.

Eating too much junk. Things such as pop tarts, Oreos, and many fast food places are either vegan or have vegan options. This isn't giving you permission to chow down to your heart's content. These foods still have incredibly high sugar, carb, and bad fat content. Treating yourself occasionally is OK, but just be mindful.

Eating too much dairy and meat substitutes. Vegan cheese and vegan meat is a huge market, but they can also be expensive. They're basically one of the biggest reasons why veganism is seen as such an expensive lifestyle, despite the fact that it actually isn't. You don't have to buy these, let's get that clear. Yes, some of them are very healthy for you, but there are better ways to get protein. Have a little, just do it in moderation, and get the nutrients that you need from dairy and meat from other sources.

Freaking out over protein. This is the number one, most annoying question I get when people ask me about veganism. How do you get your protein? Well, for one, the average person does not need nearly as much as we think we do, only about 15% of our diet, and there are plenty of other places to get it. Beans, nuts, tofu, grains, there are plenty of sources.

Not eating enough. Veggies and fruit, foods you'll likely be eating quite a lot of, are full of fiber, and fiber doesn't get digested by the system. It also helps trick you into thinking that you're full, and you've had enough. Your body is digesting foods at a faster rate. Remember, the foods you're eating now likely have a much lower calorie rate than the foods you were eating before. Be mindful of this, and be sure that you're getting enough food to keep you healthy and energized.

Beating yourself up every time you slip up. Look, everyone makes slip-ups. If you crack and buy a chicken burger after three weeks of being vegan straight, don't think that you're a horrible person. It happens. Or even if you make a mistake, accidentally buying something that isn't vegan. Maybe the burger is vegan, but not the bun. Maybe the pasta and pasta sauce is vegan, but not the drink that came with it. I once saw a girl burst into tears because she didn't realize that Caesar salad dressing often has anchovy paste and eggs. Be gentle on yourself, and learn for next time. This is what you'll be doing for the first little while, after all; you'll be learning. You can't be aware of everything.

Not doing the vegan lifestyle for you, or doing it for the wrong reasons. I always say that before you make a huge lifestyle change, you should have more than one reason. You should also be careful to consider that you may be feeling pressured into doing this. Are you? Are a lot of your friends vegan? Are you feeling guilty about your impact on the environment through your food? Do you want to lose weight? Have a few real, solid reasons. Maybe they're listed in our list above, maybe not. But regardless, write them down, and pull them out to remind yourself when you feel yourself going weak. Do this for you, not anybody else.

Not doing it the way that works for you. I think one of the biggest misconceptions about a new lifestyle is that it has to change right away, overnight. I think taking small steps is a much smarter way of doing it, and there's no shame in it. If you think going completely cold turkey is what works for you, then you should do that. But if you feel that slowly easing animal products out of your life by replacing one product at a time (for example, one week you could buy tofu instead of chicken, then the next week you buy tofu and plant-based milk instead of regular milk), then you should do that. You should approach this diet the way that you feel you will succeed at it.

That actually brings us into our following topic; meal prepping, and how it can help you on your vegan journey. It may help speed up the process of feeling like a complete and confident vegan and can help you resist these moments of temptation.

Meal Prepping and the Benefits

Meal Prepping can help you in a variety of ways. Not just in veganism, but in life, in general. It can help you save money, lose weight, and reduce the amount of food you throw out every year. I'm not the only one who gets annoyed when I have to throw out food, right? We'll just count a few of the ways that meal prep will help you on this new journey, plus other parts of your life. I say that even people who aren't going vegan, and just want to make their lives easier and healthier should do meal prepping.

Let's just go into a few of the ways.

It removes a lot of risks that you'll give in.

Look, if you're someone that has eaten a lot of animal products in the past, you might find yourself seriously hankering for some of them, least the first few weeks or even months. It's almost too easy to just stumble on home, and order a large pepperoni pizza with extra cheese from the local pizzeria. After all, really, one of the last things you want to do after a long day of work is to cook. Having your meals prepped and ready for you will help stop you from making that impulse decision to just order something, because all you have to do is remove it from the fridge and pop into the microwave or oven, depending on what it is. This is huge, especially for people looking to drastically change their diet. It's a lot harder to justify picking up a huge meatball sub on the way home when you already have a ready-to-go meal waiting for you at home.

It saves time. I think cooking your meals is one of the great joys in life, but I totally get that it can be a total time-sucker, especially since we're living in a world where time really is a currency. If you're doing it every day, you could be spending two hours in the kitchen, and I know there are better things that you can do in that same amount of time. You only have to do a lot of prep work once or twice a week, and on most nights, you'll only have to clean out the container and maybe a plate or bowl.

Portion control. Regardless of whether or not you're trying to lose weight, I think we should all learn a bit about portion control. We're all guilty of maybe eating just a little bit too much on occasions, and always ending up feeling sick thanks to it. By learning about portion control, we're not only keeping our health in check but we're able to enjoy little treats and foods we love without feeling like we're going to be too sick afterward.

No need to worry about food. Diet and nutrition are considered very important, and it's something that you likely find yourself worrying about. No more. By knowing that you have healthy food at home, and you don't have to concern yourself with stressing over whether or not you're going to eat something good tonight, it's all ready for you waiting at home.

Grocery shopping becomes a seamless activity. Hands up if you've gone into a grocery store and just wandered around for an hour looking for things you might use. Not only is this a waste of money as you don't have a plan for the foods that you're getting, and you may not even use them, but it's also just a huge time waster. Nobody wants to spend that long in a grocery store. Meal prepping encourages having things like meal plans and lists, so you go in knowing exactly what you're going to get. I literally only spend about one hour grocery shopping a week, and I usually go one to three times a week. You're in and out, no issues. And, if you make a point to go at a time where the grocery store isn't full of people, like early morning when it opens, you'll be in and out even faster.

You save money. Meal prepping teaches you very quickly how much you eat in a week, and how much you need. By the time that you've done it four or five times, you'll know exactly how much of each thing you'll need for the week, so you won't buy it. Not only that, but you're keeping stock of your pantry and fridge, meaning that you won't buy anything that you know you already have at home. You're also cutting back on food waste, which will save you even more money. There are few times I am more annoyed with myself then when I have to throw out food that I intended to eat and enjoy, especially when it's expensive food.

It keeps your meals different. There are plenty of different recipes in this book, and I encourage you to try them all. Not only will this ensure you're

getting a variety of different nutrients as we

talked about above, but you also won't get bored

and discouraged. It's easy to fall into a routine of

just cooking the same thing over and over again.

Thanks again to the fact that you're always

making lists, meal prep helps you keep track of

what meals you're eating. So, you know what you

had last week, and you can choose something

different this week. While there are plenty of

vegan recipes in this book that you'll love, I

definitely recommend finding a few vegan cooking

blogs or YouTube channels and subscribing to

their email list or channel. This will constantly

introduce you to new recipes every day, and you'll

find recipes that you may not have even

considered trying until you see them there. Again, just shake things up, and you'll never be bored.

So, we've gone over why you should be meal prepping, even if you're not vegan. Now, the next chapter, we're going to actually talk all about it, from the types of meal prepping to how to make it as easy as you possibly can.

Chapter Two: Meal Prep

You've likely heard of meal prepping before. Of course, you have, you picked up this book. We already talked about in the last chapter how meal prep is a great solution to helping yourself stick to a new diet. By having your meals all ready for you at home, you run out of reasons as to why you should pick up food on the way home. Not only that, but it's just really convenient. OK, I'm done. We've already gone over all the reasons why you should be doing it. Now we're going to be talking about what steps you need to take to set yourself up for a meal prepping strategy.

First off, let's go over the types of meal prep.

Types of Meal Prep

There are several different kinds of meal prep for you to choose from. It's all about choosing what makes the most sense for you and what fits into your lifestyle.

Whole meals: This involves you basically putting all of your meals together at the beginning of the week, and doing all the portion controls, separating them out into different containers. This one is perfect for lunchtime if you take your meals to work with you, and great for people who are constantly on the go.

Ingredient prep. If you're someone who doesn't mind a bit more work and you want some more variety in your meals, I definitely recommend this option. What you do is you basically just prep all your ingredients and make different meals out of them using the same prepped ingredients.

Freezing Batch Meals: this one is perfect for anyone who really just wants to have as little hassle as possible. If you're someone who doesn't actually enjoy cooking all that much, no judgment, this one is perfect for you. Just check below for our guide on how to properly defrost.

Of course, there is no issue with doing a bit of all three. Let's say you plan on putting all your lunches together at the beginning of the week, as for your breakfasts, you'll choose to just prep the ingredients, and your dinners will be frozen and prepped ingredients combination. It's about choosing something that will 100% work for you. It's all about convenience.

Now, let's chat on how to build the kitchen toolkit of your dreams.

What Should Be In Your Kitchen

Having a well-stocked kitchen in the fridge is great, but if you don't have the utensils to actually do things with it, you're definitely stuck. Now, you likely won't need everything that's on this list. Different recipes will require different tools, and the simplest recipes will have simpler tools.

Knives: Knives are the one tool that you should never go cheap on. The better quality you can get the better. You only need three of them: a chef's knife, a serrated knife, and a paring knife. Also, never buy knives online: always be sure to hold them in your hand and test them out first so you know that they'll comfortable for you to hold.

Cutting boards: this is given if you don't want your countertops to get all scratched up. I know I don't. There are two options for cutting boards, plastic, and wood. Plastic is said to be easier to sanitize, but with them, you also get large scratches where bacteria can hide, so the wood would probably be better. Also, it's recommended that people who are cutting fruit and veggies use wood. Another thing to consider: thanks to the fact that you won't be eating animal products, you don't have to worry about cross-contamination. I would still recommend that you have at least two, one for regular use and an extra one just in case.

Pots and pans: there are a lot of basic cookware sets out there, and pick the one you think will meet your needs the best. You will probably need a small and a large skillet, a few saucepans in a variety of sizes, and maybe a stockpot. Again, ask yourself what you're going to be cooking.

Baking ware: similar to pots and pans, what you'll need depends on what you plan on cooking. Baking trays, cooling racks, maybe a muffin tin, and some baking dishes. It really all depends on what you need.

Measuring cups and spoons: This is a given. You'll need them for measuring out when you're cooking. Consider having one or two sets for when you'll inevitably lose a few of them.

Bowls: these stainless steel bowls that stack on top of each other can double as both mixing bowls and serving bowls. Bonus; you'll only have to buy a set one; they last forever.

Cooking utensils: vegetable peelers, spatulas, a rolling pin, tongs, a whisk, some wooden spoons, ladle, a cheese grater, whatever else you feel you need.

Colander: these come in a variety of different sizes, so you can choose whichever size you feel you need, but get one with the smallest holes you can find.

Get the stainless steel one: it may get dented but it will last. Plastic ones are more likely to crack.

Meal prep containers: yes, there is an entire section of the container market dedicated to meal prepping. There are even sets you can get. The best ones are always the ones that are glass. These are also the most expensive, but they're great as you can microwave them without risk of BPA, and they keep food for a long time. Plastic ones are cheaper, but not recommended.

Think of all the things on this list as a long-term investment. You'll be using a lot of the tools above for years and years and years, depending on how long you keep it up. Not only that, but there is definitely something pleasing knowing that you have a fully stocked kitchen with having everything all ready for you to use. You won't need everything in here, but carefully go through the list and stick to the basics.

Now, we're going to talk about freezing.

Your Guide to Freezing Food

No matter what kind of meal prep you do, you will likely find yourself freezing something at some point. Freezing is a great way to keep food that you love throughout the year. If you have a favorite fruit that you love to use in smoothies all year round, but you find that it's too expensive during the winter, a good idea is to buy huge amounts in bulk and freeze it to use it throughout the year.

This is why the freezer is such a useful thing for your meal prep plans. You can freeze food for months, and not have to worry about cooking or what you have in the fridge, because it's all ready for you in your freezer. Most of the time, the most work that you'll have to do is pop it out of the freezer and into a bowl or container and leave it in the fridge overnight, perfectly ready for you to chow down the next day.

The real trick to being a true master at freezing foods is to know how long something can stay in the freezer. If you don't know this, you'll end up with some pretty nasty tasting food. While things like how you intend on using the food come into play, there are just some foods that aren't meant for freezing. Water-based foods, especially, unless you plan on cooking with them. Just keep this freezer guide handy and you'll be golden.

Before we get into that, here are some essential freezing tips:

Label all your foods with what they are and how they were made and when they were made. This will help you stop the whole "what is this thing in the back of my freezer" in its tracks.

Actually use it. Too many people buy food at the market, freeze it with the intention of using it for later, and never do. It stays in their freezer until it's inedible. Plan on using something from your freezer at least once a week.

Use freezer bags. They help prevent freezer burn better than regular little plastic bags do as they're made much thicker and durable. Another thing you can do to prevent freezer burn is to be sure that there is not too much air in the bags. Remember to leave space. Especially for water-based foods like soups, broths, fruit, etc. Water-based foods tend to expand when they're frozen, so just leave a bit of room to pretend breakage.

Now, for how long something lasts in the freezer:

Produce:

Vegetables: 6 to 12 months

Fruit: 6 to 12 months

Juices and juice concentrates: 6 to 12 months

Prepared smoothies: one month

Produce not to freeze: melons, citrus (juice can be frozen, not whole fruit or segments), apples, pears, lettuce, radishes, alfalfa sprouts, potatoes (unprepared, you can freeze mashed potatoes), eggplant, mashed pumpkin, and squash

Bread and Grains:

Baked bread: three months

Unbaked bread: one month

Pizza (homemade): one to two months

Cooked pasta: three months

Cooked rice: three months

Cooked whole grains: three months

Bread and grains not to freeze: cooked quinoa, uncooked grains, uncooked pasta, cereal, cooked and raw oatmeal

Prepared Meals and Miscellaneous:

Soups: three months

Chili: three months

Stews: three months

Broth: three months

Casseroles (without eggs, meat or fish): two months

Miscellaneous not to freeze: mayonnaise, prepared deli salads (egg salad, tuna salad, macaroni salad), salad dressings

Now that we've gotten all of these things out of the way, keep this in mind: always check for freezer burn, and occasionally go through your freezer and identify what needs to be thrown out and what doesn't. Don't let yourself eat something if you're not sure. Let yourself live by the words of wisdom of a lot of mothers out there; when in doubt, throw it out.

Making a Meal Plan

There are a few things to remember as you're creating a meal prep plan. Of course, the first few times are probably not going to go all that well. You'll find yourself messing up a few times. This is totally normal. Every first time meal prepper makes a few slip-ups. What matters is that you learn from them.

Here are some things to consider before you get started in meal prepping:

How long will your food last? This is something a lot of beginner meal preppers don't think of. Most fresh food has a lasting time of about 4 to 5 days, but it can be shorter or longer depending on the meal. Some foods just don't age as well as others. There are other factors in how long your food lasts, such as things like the quality of your container and how old your fridge is. Just remember to use your common sense, and don't eat something if you're not sure. Check out the FDA guidelines for a comprehensive list of how long food lasts. But, depending on how long your food lasts, this means that you'll likely have two days in the week where you're grocery shopping and cooking, rather than just one. Plan your days carefully.

When are you going to be do doing meal prepping? As time goes on, you'll likely find it easier to prep meals, and it won't take as much time or preparation. Nowadays, I can get in and out the grocery store in about 30 minutes, and be all done cooking in about one hour in a normal day, three hours in a big overhaul when I'm making everything from soup stock to smoothie bags. But I always think ahead and plan out the week before when I'm going to be doing my meal prep. You should do this, too. At the beginning of the week, plan out the exact days you're planning on going grocery shopping and when you're cooking. This will help you become more organized and you won't be impulse shopping anymore.

How complicated are you willing to make it? If you're a beginner cook, keeping things really simple will really help you out. Even if you're not a beginner cook and you've been cooking for 10 years, keeping it simple when you first start out meal prepping will probably help you out. Don't go for the overcomplicated recipes: go for the ones that have 10 or fewer ingredients, and see if you can do some crossovers (picking recipes where they have ingredients in common). If you really want to keep it simple, consider swapping out one meal at a time. Instead of meal prepping your entire week, meal prep just a small portion of your meals.

Will I actually eat this? This is a huge one. Too many times when people start the vegan diet, they assume that they have to eat foods such as tofu, even if, no matter how it's prepared, they hate tofu. This is not true. There are tons of ways to get the nutrients that tofu offers you, such as protein, that isn't just tofu, like beans and nuts. Make sure to choose recipes that you'll actually look forward to eating.

Now, when you're making a meal prep plan, take these steps:

Make your grocery list. Go through your fridge. Go through your cupboards. Take inventory of what you have on hand, and decide what things you need to pick up if you're running low on something you always like to keep on hand. Then, go through this book, or refer to another vegan cookbook or website, and find some recipes that you want to try. You should definitely figure out what recipes you like and pick some of these. These recipes will be the ones that keep you coming back for more. If you want to, you can check out your local grocery store and see if they're having any sales or promotions that you want to get in on.

Second, go to the grocery store. Stick with your list. Don't buy anything that is off your list. I would even recommend paying with cash if you want to really commit yourself. Just focus on getting the ingredients you need and get out. Another tip on how to avoid impulse purchases is eating before you go. I always go grocery shopping either right after breakfast or in the evenings after dinner. I'm guaranteed to be full, and I'm less likely to make impulse buys. This is especially important to stick to as you probably will be getting some cravings, at least for the first little while. Don't let yourself impulse buy.

Third, come home, and get cooking. I like to get everything out of the way, but of course, it really depends on you. You may go grocery shopping, bring everything home, and then decide that you'll do all the cooking later. That's okay, too. It's all up to you, and how you want to go on this journey. Now, we're going to talk about all of the amazing meals you can make with veganism!

Chapter Three: Breakfast

Breakfast is heralded as the day's most important meal. It helps to get your metabolism going, it keeps you full until lunch so you don't binge on the office donuts, and most importantly, it's delicious! Having a filling breakfast that tastes good in the morning can really set up your day for success. It really just puts you in a better mood, a good breakfast plus that morning cup of coffee really helps put a smile on your face that will last all day. It's just a good way to set off your morning.

Unfortunately, the time we're living in really doesn't set us up for a good breakfast. The idea is to jump up, 15 minutes before you have to go, and you just decide to grab a bagel on the way to work that you chow down on in the middle of traffic. You may go an entirely different route, instead choosing to skip breakfast altogether, promising yourself that you'll have an extra big lunch. Any of this sounds familiar?

Yeah?

When you choose to go vegan, that really isn't an option anymore. Not only do many restaurants and fast food place not serve vegan-friendly options, it just doesn't feel good. That 10 AM morning slump won't happen if you dedicate yourself to having breakfast every morning. No matter what your reasons are for going vegan, I will say to all of you; EAT BREAKFAST.

The recipes in this chapter are easy to put together, delicious, and nutritional. The majority of them can be made and stored a few days in advance, so it really just means that you can grab and go, literally. Some of the recipes here are definitely the kind you can eat on the road. But I personally would recommend that you definitely take the time to eat and enjoy them, because they really are so delicious. I love them all.

Steel Cut Overnight Oats

I love oatmeal. I'm not sorry at all about it. They're full of fiber and are so good on a chilly morning where all you want is some warmth to fill your belly. Despite having a reputation for being "bland", they're really not. Thanks to the fact that the actual oatmeal has all the "bland" taste, you can add anything to it. You wouldn't eat a slice of plain bread without at least a bit of jam on it, would you? Didn't think so. Oatmeal is incredibly versatile, so you can really put anything you like on it, provided that it tastes good for you. The options below are really only suggestions. These take only about one0 minutes to put together and will last in the fridge for about 5 days, meaning that they're perfect to put together at the beginning of a work week. They can be made in a jar, which is the most popular method, but there isn't really any container that these things can't be made in.

- One-half cup steel cut oats
- Three-fourths cup plant-based milk (almond, oat, soy, your choice) or water
- One-fourth tsp vanilla extract (optional)

Stir all ingredients together in the container of your choice, and let it cool for four hours in the refrigerator. In the morning, stir them together, and enjoy. You can add a bit of milk if you mind they're not smooth enough.

Now, for toppings, as I said, there are really no limits. My favorites include:

- Maple syrup
- Apple sauce (or other fruit purees)
- Berries (blueberries, raspberries, strawberries, etc)
- Fruit (banana, mango, apple, pineapple)
- Spices (cinnamon, cardamom, nutmeg, cloves)
- Nuts (pecans, peanuts, almond, walnuts)
- Nut butters (almond butter, peanut butter)
- Seeds (pumpkin, chia, poppy)
- Zest (lemon, orange)
- Chocolate
- Coconut
- Vegan chocolate chips

You can really be creative with what you put on your oats, and it will probably take some experimentation. Go for it, I say! Pick the flavors that you enjoy and have a good time. The sky's the limit.

Make Ahead Breakfast Burritos

These are easy to make and can be stored in the freezer for up to two months. They're delicious, loaded with flavor, and full of the exact nutrition that you need to get yourself fired up for the day. When you grab one out of the freezer, simply put in your fridge for an overnight thawing and for fifteen minutes, cook them in the oven for about 15 minutes at 350.

- Salt to taste
- One-fourth tsp paprika
- One-fourth tsp chili flakes
- One-half tsp chipotle powder
- One tsp turmeric
- Two tbsp olive oil

- One package of extra firm tofu, drained and pressed

- 6 tortillas wraps

Filling

- Salsa

- Black beans

- Shredded vegan cheese (optional)

- Avocado

- Red onion

- Plus whatever other favorites you want to include!

If you haven't already pressed the tofu, now is the time to do it. Check out our section on tofu in chapter 6. Once this is all done, use medium heat to warm a large-sized pan. Add oil and tofu. Use a spatula to cut up the tofu into "scrambled egg" like pieces and add the seasoning. Cook until all of it is hot and seasoned. Warm the tortillas on very low in the oven or microwave (if they're not warm, they'll fall apart when you wrap them unless they're very, very fresh). Spread wrap on a flat surface, and add in whatever vegan toppings you wish. Wrap up the burrito as you would normally, and wrap in wax paper. Store in a container or freezer bag.

Dark Chocolate Overnight Quinoa with Raspberry

This recipe sounds complicated but is actually very simple. It could be dessert, it's so good, but I say, as a treat, why not breakfast? There's nothing stopping us from pouring sweet, sugary syrup all over our pancakes, is there? This recipe makes two servings, so be sure to divide it up so you can eat it twice over.

- Nut butter (optional)
- Cocoa nibs (optional)
- One-fourth cup raw/frozen raspberries
- Two tbsp unsweetened, raw cocoa powder
- Two tbsp chia seeds
- Based milk of your choice

- One and one-half c plant

- One-third cup quinoa flakes

- One-third cup COOKED quinoa

Mix all ingredients in a sealed container. Place in

the refrigerator for a minimum of two hours,

much better if overnight.

Meal Prep Smoothie Bags

Smoothies are perfect for sipping on your way to work, and they're healthy. They, unfortunately, come with a lot of prep work, with all the slicing and dicing, and can be a bit too much work in the morning. To make it even worse, smoothies from breakfast places are often full of sugar and will only lead to a crash mid-morning. Hopefully, you can make it easier for yourself by putting together these smoothie bags. You can buy all your fruit in bulk and do them all at the same time.

Make sure to freeze everything spread out on trays rather than freeze them in the bags. If you freeze them together in the bags, they'll stick together and you'll have a much harder time blending them, which is just a time sucker. These will last up to three months, so you got some time. Here are some combinations you can try:

Mixed Berry: one cup strawberries, one-half cup blueberries, one-half cup raspberries

Mint Chocolate Chip: a banana, one-half avocado, some cocoa nibs, one tbsp cocoa powder, one-fourth cup fresh mint, one cup spinach

Strawberry banana: one cup spinach one cup strawberries, a banana,

Tropical Green Smoothie: one cup spinach, one cup pineapple, one cup mango

Chocolate Strawberry: a banana, two c strawberries

Similar to the oatmeal, you can mix match and change what you want as you wish. It's really your choice as to what you want to have. You can also add other things like nuts, hemp seeds, nut butter, protein powder, spices, and more to give them more nutrients.

For blending, grab one of the bags out of the freezer and empty contents into a blender. Add about one cup of whatever plant-based milk you wish, but almond is the most popular. Blend on high for about one and a half minutes or until everything is blended. Grab a straw as you rush out the door and enjoy!

Vanilla Chia Pudding with Berries

This is another breakfast that could be classified as a dessert, but chia pudding is very, very good for you. Chia seeds are packed with antioxidants, protein, fiber, and omega-three acids, which is usually found in the fridge. They also don't have too many calories, despite being very filling. They're a perfect way to start your day off! Not only that, but they're super easy to make, requiring almost no effort at all.

- One-half cup berries of your choice, fresh or frozen
- One tsp Vanilla extract
- Two t chia seeds
- One-half cup plant-based milk, your choice

- One tbsp Xylitol (optional)

Mix together the milk, vanilla, and xylitol if you choose to. Pour this mixture in with the chia seeds. Do it very well, and make sure every seed is coated. Put the mixture into a container of your choice, and place in the fridge. You can add the blueberries before putting it in the fridge or after, it's your choice. This will last about 5 days in the fridge, so it's a good idea to make this in bulk.

Fluffy Flourless Banana Pancakes

The words "fluffy" and "flourless" don't generally go together, but these pancakes are amazing. The idea of anyone giving up pancakes is unfathomable. After all, they're delicious. Well, you're in luck; not only are these pancakes, but they're made with no animal products and are gluten-free, as well as having some extra nutrient packs in the form of oats and banana. Plus, they're simple to make and take very little time.

- One cup of rolled oats
- One-fourth cup of plant-based milk, your choice
- One ripe banana (the riper, the easier time you will have)

- One tbsp baking apple cider vinegar

- One tbsp baking powder

- One-half tsp cinnamon

- One tsp vanilla extract (optional)

- One tbsp maple syrup (optional)

- Whatever toppings you choose

Blend all the ingredients in a blender until smooth. Allow the batter to rest for at least 5 minutes. This step is important as it gives the oats time to soak up the liquid, and the batter will thicken. Reheat a nonstick pan. When it's hot, now it's time to make the pancakes. Take one-fourth cup of batter, and pour into the pan. Cook for about one-two minutes. Cook the other side for two minutes as well. Slide onto a plate. Do this until they're all done. Consider doubling or tripling this recipe if you want to make a meal prepping, and store them in the freezer. Put wax sheets in between them to make them easy to separate. Choose whatever vegan toppings you want.

Oat Flour Waffles with Blueberries

Waffles are another breakfast staple that nobody should have to give up, and thankfully, you don't have to. These are delicious, filled with blueberries (or really, whichever you wish, it could be replaced with vegan chocolate chips, if you want). Who doesn't love waffles?

- One cup oat flour
- One-fourth cup plant-based milk, your choice
- One-half cup applesauce, unsweetened
- One tsp vanilla extract
- One tsp lemon juice
- One tbsp baking powder

- One-fourth cup blueberries (strawberries, raspberries, and vegan chocolate chips could also be used)
- Two tbsp maple syrup (optional)
- Whatever toppings you choose

Combine everything, minus your blueberries, in a blender. Make sure to only blend until it's fully blended, and not any longer. Add your blueberries (or substitute) in, and mix for half a second once or twice, but this step is optional. Coat a waffle iron with cooking spray or oil, and pour half of the batter into it. Cook according to iron instructions. Repeat once over. This recipe will only create about two waffles, so if you want to cook in advance, consider doing the same as you would do with the pancakes and doubling or tripling the recipe to create more. This means that you'll have a lot of waffles to eat during the week. All you have to do is toss them in the microwave or in your oven or the toaster, and go. Yum!

Homemade Granola

Granola is a great healthy breakfast to enjoy on a busy morning. This one is great over plant-based yogurt with berries for a morning fruit parfait. Who doesn't love fruit parfaits? This recipe makes about 8 cups of granola, and it may be a bit time consuming, but it is SO EASY to make.

- Four cups rolled oats
- Three-fourths cup raw pecans
- Three-fourths cup walnuts
- One-half cup melted cooking oil, olive or coconut
- One-third cup pure maple syrup (you could also use honey if you want)
- One tsp vanilla extract

- One-third cup dried cranberries (blueberries, strawberries, or raspberries can serve as an option too)
- One tsp salt
- Whatever spices you wish (cinnamon, cloves, etc)
- One-half cup coconut flakes (optional)

Line a pan with parchment paper, and ensure 350 degrees is the temperature of your oven. Mix the salt, nuts, oats, and some different spices (cinnamon is wonderful) together and combine until fully mixed. Add the oil, vanilla, and maple syrup, and make sure it's completely mixed. When this is done, spread it out over your pan in an even layer. Bake for 10 minutes, then remove, mix around. Add the coconut flakes here if you plan on it, and mix again. Return to oven for 8 to 12 minutes. Check it regularly. Once it is a golden brown on top, take out of the oven. It will crisp up more once it's cooled. Add the cranberries on top. Let the granola cool completely before you start to break it up into pieces, and remove any chunks. For storage, pour into an airtight container, where it will stay fresh for about two weeks. If you want it to last a bit longer, store in the refrigerator, but it's so good that you probably won't have that issue.

Breakfast Quinoa Salad

This isn't really a meal prep meal (well, it could be, it's your choice) but this is great for when you have a brunch potluck that you have to go to in the morning. It's full of nutrition, filling, and delicious. The berries give it a sweet bite that is enjoyable and full of antioxidants. The quinoa and oats deliver a large helping of fiber and protein. It makes about 8 servings, making it perfect to bring to a friend's brunch, especially if they won't have many vegan options.

- One cup dry quinoa
- One cup steel-cut oats
- Three tbsp olive oil

- One-half cup dry millet

- One and one-inch piece fresh ginger, peeled and cut into coins

- One-half cup maple syrup

- Two large lemons

- One cup plant-based yogurt

- One-fourth tsp nutmeg

- Two cups toasted hazelnuts

- Two cups blueberries (raspberries or chopped strawberries also work)

- Salt

Mix quinoa, millet, and oats all together in a strainer. Rinse thoroughly under cold water and set aside. Over medium-high stove setting, heat the olive oil (about one teaspoon) in a saucepan. Cook the grains for two to three minutes, until they start giving off a toast-like smell. This makes your quinoa about ten times more delicious. Once this is done, add four and one-half cups of water, and stir in about three-fourths tsp salt, and the ginger. Zest one of the lemons, and add this as well. Bring the mixture to boil. Let it simmer, covered, over low heat for fifteen to twenty minutes. While this is happening, zest the other lemon, and set aside. After your quinoa mixture is done cooking, let it sit off the heat for five minutes. Use a fork to fluff it once the lid is removed. This is also the time where you would remove the ginger that you added.

If it's done cooking to the consistency that you want, let the mixture cool for about thirty minutes on a large baking sheet. Once this is done, put the remaining zest and the grains in a large bowl and stir. Whisk the juice of two lemons plus the rest of the olive oil in a separate bowl. Mix well. Add in the nutmeg, plant-based yogurt, and the maple syrup. Pour this over the quinoa mixture and mix. When every grain is well-coated, take the hazelnuts and chop them up. Stir in the hazelnuts plus the blueberries. If you want, you can add a bit more salt or seasonings of your choice. This recipe tastes the best when you let it sit; so keeping it in the fridge overnight will really marinate and bring these flavors to new heights.

And that's it, that's our breakfast chapter. All of these recipes are delicious, easy to make, and full of nutrition that will really get your engine going in the morning. Who says you need eggs, bacon, or dairy to have a good breakfast, right? Show people exactly what you're eating for breakfast, and they'll just be jealous, rather than thinking you're crazy for trying out this new lifestyle. Everyone on your morning transit route will be eyeing your breakfast with envy. Yum!

CPSIA information can be obtained
at www.ICGtesting.com
Printed in the USA
BVHW090137040521
606355BV00002B/90

9 781801 674232